Introduction

Many people strive to fulfill their talents, yet seven recurring root causes obstruct them from realising their potential - across careers, relationships, and purpose. This book examines the psychology behind these silent killers of excellence like toxic blame games, initiative inertia and delusional denial that reliably undermine performance.

Packed with excellent hints and tips to achieve success in your career, you'll learn to identify weaknesses, and challenges that may be holding you back and preventing the confidence, progress, and results that you, your team and your organisation want. Let's stop reacting to the symptoms of poor and ineffective management and address the root causes.

This is your solution.

In this book, I will introduce you to 7 archetypes of employee you may already know:

- **The Frozen**
- **The Defector**
- **The Deflector**
- **The Delusional**
- **The Uninspired**
- **The Uninformed**
- **The Self-Obsessed**

Just reading about them will <u>not</u> improve your performance:

- **However, recognise, relate, assimilate, and apply the following suggestions.**

  to get on point, on form and on fire to achieve the success you want.

 **When you see this symbol throughout the book. Pause & reflect. Make notes, Answer the Question or Complete the exercise. This will assist you.**

When it comes to your life, career, or business, it's now time to identify who is holding you back and preventing the confidence, progress, and results that you want to achieve.

Onwards and upwards

Fraser J. Hay

February 2024

Table of Contents

Introduction 1

About The Author 4

Ego (The Self-Obsessed) 5

Blame (The Defector) 13

Denial (The Delusional) 32

Ignorance (The Uninformed) 42

Apathy (The Uninspired) 51

Fear (The Frozen) 60

Thank You 70

About The Author

Fraser Hay is the founder of itstacksup.com. A marketing consultant, business coach and keynote speaker, he helps founders, business owners and managers to plan, document, automate and execute their marketing strategy.

Based 60 miles north of Aberdeen in the highlands of Scotland, Fraser has delivered keynotes on 4 continents and helped individuals and entrepreneurs in over 40 countries to identify, pursue and achieve their personal, professional, and commercial objectives.

An award-winning entrepreneur, Fraser has spent 20 years documenting over 2000 issues, challenges, obstacles, and solutions for each of the 4 stages of the entrepreneurial journey and shares them in his books, courses, keynotes, training, and consultancy.

He also provides marketing automation solutions to business owners to help reduce waste, inefficiency, and duplication of effort. His entrepreneurial systems and solutions enable owners, managers, and staff to get on point, on form and on fire to improve ROI whilst holding staff and team members accountable.

He can be contacted via his website
https://www.itstacksup.com

Ego (The Self-Obsessed)

Ego, or what I term "The Self-Obsessed," encompasses a set of detrimental tendencies that can impede productivity, collaboration, and overall success. Rooted in self-absorption, it entails an unyielding fixation on one's needs, desires, and sense of importance. This chapter delves into the intricacies of ego within organizational dynamics, exploring its multifaceted nature and profound impact.

"The Self-Obsessed" ego embodies a pervasive inclination towards self-centeredness and a fixation on personal validation and status. It manifests through behaviors like reluctance to acknowledge faults and an incessant pursuit of recognition. Such tendencies undermine collaboration, hinder innovation, and impede overall success within organizations.

This chapter aims to shed light on the origins, manifestations, and consequences of "The Self-Obsessed" ego. It often emerges as a coping mechanism against insecurities and fears, morphing into a barrier to personal growth and meaningful relationships.

Throughout this chapter, I invite readers to reflect on their experiences and tendencies shaped by ego within organizational settings. Fostering self-awareness and humility can help individuals transcend ego's limitations and embrace collaboration, empathy, and shared purpose.

What the experts say.

According to renowned psychologist Sigmund Freud, ego plays a crucial role in our psyche, balancing the demands of our primal instincts (id) and societal norms (superego). He famously stated, "The ego is not master in its own house" (Freud, 1923).

Author and speaker Eckhart Tolle offers insights into how ego can hinder our success, stating, "The ego is always on guard against any kind of perceived diminishment. To the ego, surrender means giving up power" (Tolle, 2004).

This means that when we let our ego take control, we become more focused on protecting our image and asserting our dominance rather than working towards our goals.

In simpler terms, our ego can act like a barrier, blocking us from seeing opportunities for growth and collaboration.

So, if we want to be successful, we need to learn how to keep our ego in check and be open to learning from others.

Remember, success often comes from humility and the willingness to admit when we don't have all the answers.

Have you ever experienced a situation like this?

In a marketing firm, the team is brainstorming ideas for a new ad campaign. Sarah, the creative director, often lets her ego get in the way. She believes her ideas are always the best and dismisses input from her colleagues. This behaviour stifles creativity and collaboration, leading to subpar campaign concepts.

To address this, the team leader, Alex, organises a workshop on effective communication and teamwork. Sarah learns to listen actively to her team members' ideas and encourages open discussion. As a result, the team has started generating more innovative and successful ad campaigns, boosting the firm's reputation and client satisfaction.

If not you, then maybe someone you know has experienced a situation like this:

Mark, the lead programmer in a software development company, has a big ego. He insists on implementing his coding solutions without considering input from his teammates. This leads to errors and delays in project deadlines, causing frustration among the team.

To tackle this issue, the project manager, Emily, holds a team-building retreat focused on fostering trust and collaboration. Mark learns to value his colleagues' expertise and begins to involve them in decision-making processes. With improved teamwork, the company delivers projects more efficiently, earning higher client satisfaction and increasing profitability.

My point?

In both situations, ego initially hindered team performance and organizational success. However, by implementing measures to promote collaboration and humility, individuals like Sarah and Mark were able to overcome their ego-driven behaviors and contribute positively to their teams and organisations.

In the world of personal development and understanding why people might not be at their best, "ego" is important. It's like that voice inside your head that's always saying, "Me, me, me!"

Ego can be defined as an individual's exaggerated sense of self-importance and entitlement, often manifested through a relentless need for control, recognition, and validation. It is a psychological construct that drives behaviours characterised by arrogance, dominance, and an unwillingness to consider alternative viewpoints or feedback from others. Ego blinds individuals to their own limitations, fostering a belief in their superiority and infallibility while diminishing the contributions and perspectives of their colleagues.

Ego serves as a barrier to collaboration, innovation, and effective teamwork, undermining organizational success and individual growth.

Understanding Ego and its effects.

In various industries, signs of ego affecting performance can manifest in different ways, impacting individuals, teams, and entire organisations. For instance, in a corporate setting, an individual with a strong ego may prioritize personal recognition over team success. They might refuse to collaborate with colleagues, insist on having their ideas implemented without considering others' input, and resist feedback that challenges their authority or expertise.

In the healthcare industry, ego-driven behaviour among medical professionals can lead to detrimental consequences. For instance, a doctor with a big ego may dismiss input from nurses or other healthcare staff, leading to breakdowns in communication and coordination of patient care. This can result in medical errors, compromised patient safety, and diminished trust within the healthcare team.

In the technology sector, ego-driven behaviour can hinder innovation and collaboration. For example, a software developer with a strong ego may resist incorporating feedback from testers or users, believing their code is flawless. This can lead to products failing to meet user needs or expectations, impacting customer satisfaction and the company's reputation.

Be on your guard over your own behaviour and that of colleagues. Overall, signs of ego affecting performance can include resistance to collaboration, refusal to accept feedback, prioritization of personal recognition over team success, and a lack of willingness to consider others' perspectives.

Addressing ego-related issues requires fostering a culture of humility, open communication, and collaboration within the workplace. This can involve implementing feedback mechanisms, promoting teamwork and shared goals, and providing leadership development programs that emphasize the importance of humility and empathy. By addressing ego-related issues, organizations can improve teamwork, innovation, and overall performance.

If it goes unchecked.

Imagine you're in a team working on a project, and there's this person named Alex who always needs to be the centre of attention. Alex's unchecked ego can have a big impact on the individual, the team, and the organisation.

For Alex, their ego might make them resistant to feedback or new ideas, hindering their personal growth and development. They might miss opportunities to learn and improve their skills because they're too focused on proving themselves right.

At this stage, you're wondering about the potential impact on the team. Alex's ego-driven behaviour can create tension and conflict within the team. Others might feel sidelined or undervalued, leading to decreased morale and productivity. Team members may become disengaged or even leave the team altogether, resulting in a loss of valuable talent and expertise.

Finally, consider the impact on the organisation. A team that's divided by ego-driven conflicts is less likely to achieve its goals effectively. Projects might be delayed or fail to meet expectations, leading to financial losses and damage to the organization's reputation. Additionally, a toxic work environment fueled by unchecked egos can hinder innovation and collaboration, putting the organization at a disadvantage compared to competitors.

For me, an unchecked ego can have far-reaching consequences on both individuals and organizations. It's important for everyone in the workplace to recognize the negative impact of ego-driven behavior and work towards fostering a culture of humility, respect, and collaboration.

Potential Solutions

To prevent ego from causing problems in the workplace, there are several preventative measures, systems, and processes that individuals, teams, and organisations can put in place:

1. Promote humility. Encourage individuals to stay humble and recognize that they don't have all the answers. This can be done through training sessions, workshops, or even team discussions focused on the importance of humility.

2. Encourage listening. Emphasise the importance of active listening within teams and organizations. Encourage individuals to listen to others' perspectives without interrupting or dismissing them, fostering a culture of mutual respect.

3. Acknowledge contributions. Ensure that everyone's contributions are recognized and valued, regardless of their position or level of seniority. This helps prevent individuals from feeling the need to assert their egos to gain recognition.

4. Establish clear goals. Set clear goals and expectations for individuals and teams, ensuring that everyone understands their role in achieving them. This helps keep the focus on collective success rather than individual accomplishments.

5. Provide feedback. Create a culture where feedback is given and received openly and constructively. This allows individuals to receive feedback on their behavior and performance, helping them recognize and address any ego-driven tendencies.

6. Encourage collaboration. Promote teamwork and collaboration within teams and across departments. Encourage individuals to work together towards common goals, fostering a sense of camaraderie and shared purpose.

7. Lead by example. Leaders should model humility and collaboration in their own behaviour, setting a positive example for others to follow. When leaders prioritise teamwork and mutual respect, it sends a clear message that ego-driven behavior is not acceptable.

By implementing these preventative measures, individuals, teams, and organisations can create a positive and supportive work environment where ego is kept in check, and everyone can thrive and succeed together.

Ask Yourself

Take a moment to ask yourself the following questions and confirm whether you recognise yourself (or any member of your team or organisation):

- Do I often feel the need to be the center of attention in personal situations, or am I able to listen and appreciate the contributions of others?

- In my professional life, do I prioritize my own success and recognition over the success of the team or organization, or do I work collaboratively towards shared goals?

- When making decisions in commercial endeavours, do I consider the perspectives and input of others, or do I insist on my own way without regard for alternative viewpoints?

- How do I react when faced with feedback or criticism? Do I become defensive and dismissive, or do I approach it with an open mind and willingness to learn and improve?

- In team settings, am I supportive of my colleagues' achievements and successes, or do I feel threatened and insecure when others excel?

- When evaluating commercial opportunities or partnerships, do I prioritize my own interests and ego, or do I consider what is best for the overall success of the venture?

- How do I handle conflicts or disagreements in personal, professional, or commercial situations?

- Do I let my ego drive my actions and decisions, or do I approach them with humility and a focus on finding mutually beneficial solutions?

Reflecting on these questions can help individuals gain insight into their ego-driven tendencies and their impact on personal, professional, and commercial situations. It can also guide them towards fostering a more collaborative and inclusive approach in their interactions and decision-making processes.

	**Q. Is ego a cause that is preventing you, your team, department, or organisation from being effective?**

1. No, I don't know anyone like that in my team or organsiation

2. Yes. It has been identified in the relevant individual(s).

3. On the case. Working to address it and improve effectiveness.

4. Oops. No, the action plan is not yet completed (or started).

5. This is concerning. I Need help with this – fast.

Blame (The Defector)

Blame, or "The Defector" as I call it, is the tendency to not take responsibility for one's circumstances and instead point the finger at others. When we blame, we act as though we are merely helpless victims of external forces and other people's shortcomings. We refuse ownership of our predicaments.

For example, if an employee misses a deadline, a blame response would be "my manager didn't give me clear directions" or "my co-workers didn't do their parts to help me." There is no self-reflection or accountability. The blame deflects onto others.

Blame strips us of creative power and the ability to learn. When we fault external indivudals, situations or events, we excuse our own need for improvement. We also damage relationships and trust by constantly accusing others. This makes it difficult to work together towards positive change.

The blame mentality holds us back from growth, problem-solving, accountability, and leadership. It locks us into ineffectiveness while protecting the ego from the vulnerability of self-reflection. I term it "The Defector" because it defects responsibility onto anyone and anything but oneself.

Of the seven causes of human ineffectiveness, few are as widespread and stealthily toxic as the tendency to pass blame. When we point fingers outward instead of inward, we become experts at rationalising our own shortcomings while villainizing the faults of others. We morph into helpless victims, outraged at the injustices being perpetrated against us. Our creative power evaporates behind an impenetrable shield of self-defence mechanisms designed to avoid the discomfort of accountability.

In this chapter we will unpack the psychological drivers of blame, its self-sabotaging consequences, and strategies for transcending fault-finding and victimhood. By learning to drop the poisoning reflex to pass blame outward at any hint of failure or frustration, we reclaim our latent potency and flexibility.

We evolve from captured pawns on life's chessboard into self-determining kings and queens who understand the true nature of power. Accountability sets us free.

What the experts say

"Blame is a common barrier to success because it shifts our focus away from solutions and keeps us stuck in a cycle of negativity," notes Dr. Brene Brown, a research professor and author of "The Gifts of Imperfection." She elaborates, "When we blame others for our problems, we give away our power to change our circumstances." In simpler terms, blaming others prevents us from taking responsibility for our actions and finding constructive ways to address challenges.

This can hinder our progress and limit our potential for growth. Dr. Brown emphasizes the importance of cultivating empathy and accountability, stating that "taking ownership of our mistakes and learning from them is essential for personal and professional development." By adopting a mindset of self-reflection and accountability, we can overcome the barrier of blame and strive towards greater success and fulfilment.

Have you ever experienced situations like these before?

Have you or anyone you know been in a scenario where blame can negatively impact individuals, teams, and the organisations?

For example, Meet Wendy.

She is a marketing manager at a retail company. During a campaign launch, a mistake occurs in the promotional materials, leading to customer complaints and decreased sales. Instead of taking responsibility, Wendy blames her team members for not proofreading the content properly.

This causes resentment among the team, as they feel unfairly targeted for Wendy's mistake. The blame game leads to decreased morale and productivity, hindering the team's ability to address the issue effectively.

To correct this situation, the company's leadership intervenes and facilitates a team meeting to address the issue. They emphasise the importance of collective accountability and encourage open communication. Wendy apologises to her team and acknowledges her role in the mistake, fostering a culture of transparency and trust.

Moving forward, the team implements a thorough review process for all promotional materials, ensuring that mistakes are caught before they impact sales.

Now, let's consider John.

He is a project manager at a software development company. During a crucial project deadline, a bug is discovered in the code, causing delays and client dissatisfaction. Instead of taking responsibility, John blames his team members for not coding properly. This creates tension within the team, as members feel demoralized and unfairly criticized for John's oversight. The blame game leads to decreased collaboration and innovation, jeopardizing the success of future projects.

To correct this situation, the company's leadership conducts a performance review and identifies areas for improvement in project management practices. John undergoes training on effective leadership and communication skills, learning to take responsibility for mistakes and provide constructive feedback to his team.

Additionally, the team implements a peer review process for code development, fostering collaboration and accountability among team members.

My point?

Through these actions, the team overcomes the barrier of blame and works together towards achieving their goals effectively.

Blame is the act of holding others responsible for undesirable circumstances that one faces. When we play the "blame game", we point the finger outwards rather than inwards. We refuse to be accountable for outcomes, preferring to position ourselves as victims wronged by people or events. Metaphorically, blame is like defective eyesight - we see faults in everyone except ourselves.

The instinct to blame often stems from psychological drivers like:

Fear of failure - accepting responsibility may reveal our flaws or inadequacies. Ego protection mechanisms shift the focus onto scapegoats.

Lack of internal locus of control - a worldview where we believe things happen to us rather than through us. We lack agency.

Cognitive dissonance - when our self-image of competence doesn't match reality, it's easier to justify failure via external factors than face our shortcomings.

Learned behaviour - some adopt a victimhood mentality as a convenient strategy to avoid accountability if they grow up exposed to blame culture.

Understanding Blame and its effects

Let's delve into how blame can negatively impact individuals, teams, and organisations in the workplace.

Denise was a project manager at a construction company. When a project deadline was missed due to unforeseen delays, Denise immediately pointed fingers at her team members, blaming them for not working efficiently.

This created tension within the team as members felt unfairly targeted and demoralised. Instead of working together to find solutions, the team became divided, hindering productivity and progress on future projects. The organisation also suffers from decreased client satisfaction and reputational damage due to missed deadlines and poor teamwork.

Now, let's shift our focus to Paul, a sales executive at a software company. When sales numbers declined, John blamed external factors like market conditions or lack of marketing support, refusing to take any responsibility for his own performance.

This created a culture of finger-pointing within the sales team, where individuals felt discouraged and disempowered. As a result, sales performance continued to decline, impacting the organisation's revenue and growth prospects.

In both situations, blame negatively affected individuals, teams, and organisations by creating a toxic work environment characterised by low morale, decreased productivity, and damaged relationships.

To address this issue, it's essential for individuals like Denise and John to recognise the impact of their blame-driven behaviour and work towards fostering a culture of accountability, collaboration, and problem-solving within their teams and organisations.

Left unchecked, chronic blame games within teams severely undermine organisational effectiveness through cultural toxicity. Trust and psychological safety erode amidst endless finger-pointing politics stifling transparency about business issues. Staff hide mistakes rather than ask for help early.

Firmly addressing the predictable toxicity of blame games early is vital for organisations aspiring high performance continuity across market cycles, rather than ones perennially reactionary lurching crisis to crisis with more baggage accumulated each time.

If it goes unchecked

Unchecked blame can have significant negative impacts on individuals, teams, and organisations.

Firstly, let's consider the individual level. When someone is constantly blamed for mistakes or problems, it can damage their self-esteem and confidence. They may feel demoralised, unappreciated, and unwilling to take risks or contribute ideas. Over time, this can lead to decreased motivation and job satisfaction, impacting their overall performance and well-being.

At the team level, unchecked blame can create a toxic work environment characterised by low morale and high turnover. Team members may become distrustful of one another, leading to strained relationships and communication breakdowns. Collaboration suffers as individuals prioritize protecting themselves from blame rather than working together towards common goals. This can result in decreased productivity, missed deadlines, and poor-quality work.

Organisationally, unchecked blame can have serious ramifications on the company's reputation and bottom line. High turnover rates and low morale among employees can damage the organisation's employer brand, making it difficult to attract and retain top talent. Additionally, constant finger-pointing and blame-shifting can erode trust with clients and stakeholders, leading to lost business opportunities and revenue.

Overall, unchecked blame can create a negative cycle of dysfunction within the workplace, hindering individual, team, and organisational success. It's crucial for organizations to address blame culture head-on by promoting accountability, fostering open communication, and encouraging a supportive and collaborative work environment.

Potential Solutions

To prevent blame from going unchecked in the workplace, here are seven preventative measures, actions, and solutions:

1. **Promote a culture of accountability.** Encourage individuals to take ownership of their actions and decisions. Emphasize that mistakes are opportunities for learning and growth rather than reasons for blame.

2. **Establish clear communication channels.** Create open lines of communication where team members feel comfortable discussing issues and providing feedback without fear of reprisal.

3. **Encourage collaboration.** Foster a collaborative environment where individuals work together towards common goals. Emphasize the importance of supporting one another and celebrating collective successes.

4. **Lead by example.** Managers and leaders should model accountability and transparency in their own behaviour. Demonstrate willingness to take responsibility for mistakes and provide constructive feedback rather than assigning blame.

5. **Implement a no-blame policy.** Establish a formal policy or guideline that explicitly prohibits blaming others for mistakes or problems. Encourage problem-solving and purposeful discussions instead.

6. **Provide conflict resolution training.** Offer training programs or workshops on conflict resolution and effective communication skills. Equip team members with strategies for addressing conflicts constructively and resolving issues collaboratively.

7. **Celebrate successes,** Recognise, and reward achievements at both the individual and team levels. By focusing on positive outcomes, you can create a culture that values collaboration and teamwork over blame.

By implementing these preventative measures, individuals, teams, and organisations can create a positive and supportive work environment where blame is minimised, and everyone feels empowered to take responsibility for their actions and work together towards shared goals.

Ask yourself:

Take a moment to ask yourself (or members of your team) the following questions about blame to help evaluate your personal, professional, and commercial situations:

- Do I tend to blame others when things go wrong, or do I take responsibility for my own actions and decisions?
- Am I quick to assign blame to colleagues or external factors when projects don't go as planned, or do I focus on finding solutions and learning from mistakes?
- When facing challenges in my commercial endeavors, do I look for opportunities to improve and adapt, or do I point fingers at others for setbacks?
- How do I react when someone blames me for a mistake

or problem? Do I become defensive and shift blame, or do I acknowledge my role and work towards resolution?

- In team settings, am I part of a blame culture where individuals are quick to criticise and point fingers, or do we foster a supportive environment where mistakes are viewed as learning opportunities?
- When evaluating commercial partnerships or collaborations, do I consider how blame is addressed and managed within the organisation, or do I overlook this aspect and focus solely on outcomes?
- How do I handle disagreements or conflicts in personal, professional, or commercial settings? Do I resort to blame and finger-pointing, or do I approach them with empathy and a focus on finding common ground?

Reflecting on these questions can help individuals gain insight into their approach to blame and its impact on personal, professional, and commercial situations. It can also guide them towards fostering a more positive and constructive mindset in dealing with challenges and conflicts.

Q. Is "Blame" a cause that is preventing you, your team, department, or organisation from being effective?

1. No, I don't know anyone like that in my team or organsiation

2. Yes. It has been identified in the relevant individual(s).

3. On the case. Working to address it and improve effectiveness.

4. Oops. No, the action plan is not yet completed (or started).

5. This is concerning. I Need help with this – fast.

Excuses (The Deflector)

Excuses, or "The Deflector" as I term it, refer to the tendency to evade accountability for poor results by finding convenient justifications. When we make excuses, we downplay personal responsibility for outcomes by blaming situational factors - real or imagined.

For instance, if an employee misses a critical deadline, typical excuse responses would be "I had too many other priorities", "my computer crashed", or "no one told me this had become urgent." There is no ownership of the failure, just finger-pointing at other reasons.

Making chronic excuses keeps us trapped in a cycle of rationalization and defensiveness. We deflect critiques or pressures to improve performance by habitually explaining away negative feedback. There is always a ready excuse handy to preserve ego and avoid vulnerability.

This constant self-preservation reflex severely limits development of emotional intelligence, introspective muscles, and accountability. It breeds stale mindsets resistant to change and personal evolution. We get so stuck in excuse-making loops that we block out reality checks necessary for wisdom.

Just like "The Defector" of blame, excuses short-circuit effectiveness.

Of the seven root causes sabotaging human potential and businesses today, the reflex to make excuses is particularly insidious. Excuse-making allows us to constantly rationalize away our shortcomings and failures behind a smokescreen of arbitrary justifications. We motion to exonerate ourselves from any situation by playing victim and finger-pointing outwards. "It's not my fault, it's because..." is the endless litany protecting our fragile egos.

This endless spiral of evasion stunts growth. It bars wisdom gained from objectively assessing where we fall short. Social psychologist M. Scott Peck aptly called excuses "lies we tell ourselves". They prevent maturation. In this chapter, we will diagnose the psychology of excuse-making, its toxic impacts, and most importantly - treat the disease using practical techniques to restore accountability and ownership. Reality can be confronted - when excuses end, true learning begins, and potential is unlocked.

What the experts say

Excuses can hinder our success by shifting blame away from ourselves and preventing personal growth. As motivational speaker and author, Jim Rohn, once said, "If you really want to do something, you'll find a way. If you don't, you'll find an excuse."

This insight underscores the notion that excuses often stem from a lack of commitment or determination to overcome challenges. When we resort to making excuses, we relinquish control over our circumstances and allow external factors to dictate our fate.

This mindset limits our potential and prevents us from seizing opportunities for growth and achievement. Instead, we should adopt a mindset of accountability and resilience, recognizing that obstacles are simply temporary setbacks on the path to success.

As bestselling author and entrepreneur, Tony Robbins, once stated, "It's not about the resources you have, but the resourcefulness you bring to the table."

In his book "The Success Principles," Jack Canfield emphasises the detrimental impact of excuses on our journey to success, stating, "99% of all failures come from people who have a habit of making excuses." This powerful insight highlights how excuses can become ingrained habits that hold us back from achieving our goals. When we constantly make excuses, we shift the blame away from ourselves and fail to take responsibility for our actions.

By taking ownership of our actions and embracing challenges head-on, we can break free from the cycle of excuses and realize our full potential.

Ever experienced a situation like these?

Meet Colin, a project manager at a marketing agency. When a crucial client presentation is scheduled, he fails to deliver the necessary materials on time, citing unexpected technical difficulties as the reason. This leads to frustration among team members, as they had been diligently working to meet the deadline. Instead of taking ownership of her oversight, Colin continues to make excuses, blaming external factors for the delay. As a result, the client presentation is poorly executed, damaging the agency's reputation and jeopardising future business opportunities.

To address this situation, Colin's supervisor holds a team meeting to discuss the importance of accountability and communication. Colin is encouraged to take responsibility for her actions and provide realistic timelines for project deliverables in the future. Additionally, the team implements a project management tool to track progress and identify potential roadblocks proactively.

By fostering a culture of transparency and accountability, the team works together more effectively to meet client expectations and prevent future excuses.

Now, let's consider John, a sales representative at a pharmaceutical company.

When quarterly sales targets were missed, John attributed the shortfall to market volatility and increased competition. Instead of reassessing his sales strategies and prospecting efforts, John continued to blame external factors for his underperformance.

This created tension within the sales team, as members feel demoralised and frustrated by John's lack of accountability. As a result, overall sales performance continued to decline, impacting the company's revenue and market share.

To address this situation, the company's sales manager conducted individual coaching sessions with John to identify areas for improvement and develop a tailored action plan.

John received training on effective sales techniques and prospecting strategies to enhance his performance. Additionally, the sales team underwent team-building exercises to foster collaboration and support among members.

My Point?

By addressing John's excuses and providing targeted support, the sales team regained momentum and achieved its sales targets, contributing to the organisation's success.

For me, excuses refer to reasons or justifications we offer to exonerate ourselves after unfavourable outcomes. They shift accountability away from us onto other people or circumstances. Excuses act like Teflon coating - preventing cumulative life feedback from sticking to and informing our decisions.

Understanding Excuses and their effect

In a work environment, signs that excuses are affecting

performance can manifest in many ways, impacting individuals, teams, and the organisation. Individually, an employee may consistently miss deadlines and fail to deliver on their commitments, often citing external factors such as lack of resources or time constraints.

They may also demonstrate a reluctance to take on new challenges or responsibilities, using excuses to avoid stepping out of their comfort zone.

Within a team, excuses can lead to a culture of blame-shifting and finger-pointing, where members are quick to deflect responsibility for failures onto others. This can erode trust and collaboration, as team members become hesitant to take risks or share ideas for fear of being criticized or blamed. As a result, team morale and cohesion suffer, impacting productivity and hindering the achievement of collective goals.

At the organisational level, excuses may contribute to a lack of accountability and a failure to meet targets or objectives.

Leaders may encounter resistance from employees who are unwilling to take ownership of their actions or decisions, leading to stagnation and missed opportunities for growth. Additionally, excuses can damage the organisation's reputation and credibility, as clients and stakeholders may perceive it as unreliable or unprofessional.

Overall, signs of excuses affecting performance in a work environment include missed deadlines, blame-shifting, decreased morale, and failure to meet organizational objectives. Recognising these signs is essential for addressing underlying issues and fostering a culture of accountability and responsibility within the organization.

If it goes unchecked

When excuses go unchecked in a work environment, they can

have significant impact on individuals, teams, and the organisation. Individually, employees who consistently make excuses may fail to grow and develop in their roles, hindering their professional advancement and limiting their potential for success. They may also become disengaged and demotivated, as they feel justified in avoiding responsibility for their actions.

Within a team, unchecked excuses can lead to a breakdown in trust and collaboration. Team members may become resentful towards those who consistently make excuses, leading to interpersonal conflicts and reduced cohesion. This can hamper teamwork and communication, affecting the team's ability to achieve its goals and deliver results.

At the organisational level, unchecked excuses can result in missed deadlines, decreased productivity, and overall inefficiency. Leaders may struggle to hold employees accountable for their actions, leading to a lack of accountability and poor performance across the organization. Additionally, unchecked excuses can damage the organization's reputation and credibility, as clients and stakeholders may perceive it as unreliable or unprofessional.

Overall, the unchecked use of excuses in a work environment can have far-reaching consequences, impacting individual growth, team dynamics, and organizational success. It is essential for leaders to address excuses proactively and foster a culture of accountability and responsibility within the organisation.

Potential Solutions

Preventing excuses from arising or going unchecked in a work environment is crucial for fostering accountability and achieving success. Here are seven preventative measures, actions, and solutions that individuals, teams, or organizations can implement:

1. **Establish clear expectations.** Clearly define roles, responsibilities, and expectations for all team members to minimise confusion and ambiguity.
2. **Encourage open communication.** Create an environment where team members feel comfortable discussing challenges and seeking help without fear of judgment or reprisal.
3. **Set realistic goals.** Ensure that goals and targets are achievable and aligned with the team's capabilities and resources to reduce the likelihood of excuses.
4. **Provide support and resources.** Offer training, tools, and resources to help team members succeed in their roles and overcome obstacles.
5. **Lead by example.** Demonstrate accountability and integrity in your own actions and decisions, setting a positive example for others to follow.
6. **Foster a positive culture.** Promote a culture of transparency, collaboration, and continuous improvement, where mistakes are viewed as opportunities for learning and growth.
7. **Address issues promptly.** Take swift action to address excuses or poor performance, providing constructive feedback and support to help individuals overcome challenges and improve.

By implementing these preventative measures, individuals, teams, or organisations can create a supportive and accountable work environment where excuses are minimised, and everyone is empowered to take ownership of their actions and strive for excellence.

Ask yourself:

Take a moment to ask yourself (or members of your team) the following questions about excuses to help evaluate your personal, professional, or commercial situation:

- Do I find myself frequently making excuses for why I haven't achieved my personal goals or commitments?
- In my professional life, am I prone to blaming external factors or circumstances for my lack of progress or success?
- Do I often make excuses to avoid taking on new challenges or stepping out of my comfort zone?
- When faced with setbacks or failures, do I tend to make excuses rather than taking responsibility for my actions?
- Do I find myself using excuses to justify procrastination or avoid difficult tasks?
- In commercial endeavors, am I quick to attribute business challenges or failures to external factors rather than examining my own contributions or decisions?
- How do I react when others challenge or question the validity of my excuses? Am I defensive or open to constructive feedback?

Reflecting on these questions can help individuals gain insight into their tendency to make excuses and how it may be impacting their personal, professional, and commercial endeavors. It can also guide them towards adopting a more accountable and proactive mindset in addressing challenges and pursuing their goals.

Q. Are "Excuses," a cause that is preventing you, your team, department, or organisation from being effective?

1. No, I don't know anyone like that in my team or organsiation

2. Yes. It has been identified in the relevant individual(s).

3. On the case. Working to address it and

improve effectiveness.

4. Oops. No, the action plan is not yet completed (or started).

5. This is concerning. I Need help with this – fast.

Denial (The Delusional)

Denial, or "The Delusional" as I term it, refers to the rejection of truths that contradict the image of oneself or situations that one prefers to believe in. When confronted by evidence that makes us uncomfortable, denial triggers defence mechanisms to brush off, downplay and distort objective reality to protect the ego.

For example, if a leader refuses to acknowledge declining revenue trends, mounting customer dissatisfaction and realities about market share loss, they have slipped into denial. Despite data, they filter information in biased ways saying, "the fundamentals are still strong" or "these are just temporary external issues." They retreat from truth into delusional thinking.

This inability to factually diagnose problems pushes solutions endlessly further away. Change gets stonewalled when denial sets in among decision makers unwilling to confront harsh truths starring in their face. They remain passive bystanders across an increasingly diverging gap between their preferred worldview and ground realities. Stress piles as cognitive dissonance builds inside from the mental gymnastics necessary to constantly explain away evidence contrary to one's beliefs and assumptions.

Unchecked, denial results in disaster down the road when entrenched attitudes refuse course correction despite obvious warning signals. Leaders living within subjective bubbles of their preferences, biases and filter bubbles lose touch. They fly an airborne plane never realizing that the fuel is about to run out. That crash is inevitable before finally jolting them awake from their deluded slumber. But by then, it is too late, and consequences are dramatic.

Denial distorts the lenses through which we view reality. When left untreated by an insistence on dogmatically wearing rose-tinted glasses, the delusion deepens. We stray ever further from truth, objectivity, and pragmatic solutions. As Henry David Thoreau warned - "Rather than love, than money, than fame, give me truth." Denial forsakes truth by covering up inconvenient facts that require mature coping. By facing reality with courage and responsibility, denial gives way to dealing effectively with what lies before us.

Simply put, the path of least resistance is often to deny the truth rather than adjust expectations. By rejecting inconvenient facts starring us in the face, we enter a state of delusion that allows us to keep living in subjective bubbles of our own preferences.

While this may present short-term comfort by avoiding the pains of facing difficult truths, overall denial exacts heavy costs. Failures get compounded when problems don't get addressed early since accompanying warning signs got brushed aside.

In this chapter, we will anatomise the slippery mechanism of denial, study its immense damage potential, and equip you the reader with tactics to recognise and counter denial's allure. For leaders and teams living in truth is the ultimate competitive advantage.

What the experts say

Denial, as described by bestselling author and psychiatrist M. Scott Peck, can function as a significant barrier to success by preventing individuals from acknowledging and addressing their problems. Peck famously stated, "The truth is that our finest moments are most likely to occur when we are feeling deeply uncomfortable, unhappy, or unfulfilled."

This insight underscores the importance of confronting uncomfortable truths rather than denying or avoiding them. When individuals deny their challenges or shortcomings, they hinder their ability to learn, grow, and overcome obstacles.

Instead of facing reality and taking initiative-taking steps towards improvement, they remain stuck in a cycle of stagnation and mediocrity. By embracing discomfort and accepting the truth, individuals can break free from denial's grip and pave the way for personal and professional success.

Have you ever experienced a situation like these?

I recall lady called Angela a marketing manager in an IT firm. Despite declining sales figures and negative customer feedback, she adamantly denied that there were any issues with the marketing strategies she implemented. She insisted that the market conditions were to blame and refused to acknowledge any shortcomings in her approach. As a result, the company's revenue continued to decline, and morale among the sales team plummeted.

Worse, the company's CEO initiated a comprehensive review of the marketing strategies and performance metrics. The findings revealed that Angela's denial had indeed contributed to the company's poor performance. The CEO then implemented corrective measures, including reevaluating the marketing strategies, providing additional training for Angela and her team, and fostering a culture of openness and accountability.

With these actions in place, the marketing team was able to identify and address the shortcomings in their approach, leading to improved sales performance and a revitalized company. In some organisations however, she might not have been given a second chance.

Now, do you know someone who's experienced a situation like this?

Angus was an engineering manager in a construction company. Despite numerous warnings from team members about potential safety hazards on a construction site, Angus dismissed their concerns and continued with the project without implementing proper safety measures. Unfortunately for Angus, his denial led to a serious workplace accident, resulting in injuries to several workers and considerable damage to the company's reputation.

To rectify the situation, the company conducted a thorough investigation into the accident, which revealed Angus 's negligence and denial of safety concerns.

My point?

As a result, Angus was removed from his managerial position, and the company implemented stricter safety protocols and training for all employees. Additionally, the company emphasised the importance of initiative-taking safety measures and encouraged a culture where employees felt empowered to speak up about safety concerns without fear of reprisal. These actions helped prevent future accidents and fostered a safer work environment for all employees.

For me, Denial, refers to the psychological defence mechanism where individuals refuse to accept reality or acknowledge the truth of a situation. It involves blocking out or minimizing uncomfortable thoughts, feelings, or facts that may challenge one's beliefs or self-image.

In simpler terms, denial is like wearing blinders to avoid facing inconvenient truths or uncomfortable realities. It can manifest in various aspects of life, such as personal relationships, professional challenges, or health issues. Individuals in denial may dismiss evidence or feedback that contradicts their beliefs, making it difficult for them to recognise and address problems. Denial can hinder personal growth, prevent effective problem-solving, and lead to detrimental consequences if left unchecked.

Understanding Denial and its effects

Let's explore how it can affect an individual, the team, and the whole organization:

Someone in denial might brush off feedback or constructive criticism, saying, "I'm doing just fine," even when they're not. They might blame others for their mistakes instead of taking responsibility. For example, if a project fails, they might blame it on external factors rather than examining their own contribution.

They may avoid facing problems or challenges, pretending everything is okay when it's not. For instance, they might procrastinate on important tasks rather than addressing them.

Team Impact:

In a team setting, a person in denial might resist collaborating or sharing information, thinking they don't need help. Others in the team may feel frustrated or demotivated when working with someone who refuses to acknowledge issues or mistakes.

The team might miss valuable opportunities for improvement or innovation because the person in denial refuses to consider alternative perspectives. When denial permeates the workplace, overall performance can suffer as problems go unaddressed and mistakes are repeated.

A culture of denial can spread throughout the organisation, hindering openness, honesty, and accountability. Employees may lose trust in leadership if they perceive a lack of willingness to acknowledge and address problems.

Denial can act like fog, clouding judgment and hindering progress. It's essential for individuals, teams, and organisations to recognise and address it to foster a healthy and productive work environment.

If it goes unchecked.

If Denial creeps into the workplace, it can cause all sorts of problems if left unchecked. Here's how it can wreak havoc on individuals, teams, and the entire organization:

- **Stunted Growth.** When someone denies their mistakes or shortcomings, they miss valuable opportunities for personal and professional growth. Without acknowledging areas needing improvement, they remain stuck in the same spot.

- **Career Damage.** Continuously denying feedback or refusing to address issues can harm an individual's reputation and hinder their career progression. They may miss promotions or even face disciplinary actions.

- **Dysfunctional Dynamics.** In a team environment, unchecked denial can lead to dysfunctional dynamics where trust erodes, collaboration suffers, and communication breaks down. This can create tension and conflict among team members.

- **Decreased Productivity.** When team members refuse to acknowledge problems or mistakes, productivity takes a hit. Instead of focusing on solutions, time and energy are wasted on avoiding or covering up issues.

- **Cultural Decay.** A pervasive culture of denial can poison the organizational culture, fostering an environment where accountability is scarce, and transparency is non-existent. This can lead to a toxic workplace culture where employees feel disengaged and undervalued.

- **Loss of Competitive Edge.** Organisations that fail to address denial risk falling behind competitors. Without a culture that encourages learning from mistakes and adapting to change, innovation stagnates, and the company becomes less competitive in the market.

Potential Solutions.

Here are seven simple ways individuals, teams, or organisations can prevent denial from causing trouble:

1. **Encourage Open Communication:** Foster an environment where people feel comfortable sharing concerns, feedback, and mistakes without fear of judgment.

2. **Provide Constructive Feedback.** Offer feedback in a respectful and constructive manner, focusing on solutions rather than blame.

3. **Promote Self-Reflection.** Encourage individuals to reflect on their actions and behaviours regularly, fostering self-awareness and accountability.

4. **Lead by Example.** Leaders should demonstrate openness and willingness to acknowledge mistakes, setting a positive example for others to follow.

5. **Establish Clear Expectations.** Ensure everyone understands expectations and goals, reducing ambiguity and the likelihood of denial when things go off track.

6. **Implement Regular Check-ins.** Schedule regular meetings or check-ins to review progress, address challenges, and provide support where needed.

7. **Celebrate Learning Moments.** Instead of focusing solely on success, celebrate learning moments and the lessons gained from setbacks, reinforcing a growth mindset.

By implementing these preventative measures, individuals, teams, and organisations can create a culture that values honesty, accountability, and continuous improvement, reducing the risk of denial taking hold and causing harm.

Unchecked denial can act like a slow-burning fire, gradually eroding morale, productivity, and the success of the organization. It's crucial for individuals, teams, and organizations to confront and address denial head-on to foster a culture of honesty, accountability, and continuous improvement.

Ask yourself:

Take a moment to ask yourself (or members of your team) the following questions about "Denial" to help evaluate your personal, professional, or commercial situation:

- Am I open to acknowledging my mistakes and weaknesses, or do I tend to brush them aside?
- Do I seek feedback from others to understand areas where I can improve, or do I dismiss criticism?
- Am I willing to take responsibility for my actions, or do I often blame others when things go wrong?
- Do I actively seek opportunities for professional development and growth, or do I resist change and new challenges?
- Am I honest with myself and my colleagues about my

capabilities and limitations, or do I pretend to know everything?

- Do I address problems and conflicts in the workplace head-on, or do I avoid them and hope they'll go away?
- Is my business open to feedback from customers and clients, or do we ignore complaints and negative reviews?
- Are we willing to adapt our products or services based on market feedback, or do we cling to outdated strategies?
- Do we acknowledge our competitors' strengths and weaknesses, or do we underestimate them, and risk being blindsided?

These questions can help you assess whether denial might be impacting your personal growth, professional success, or business effectiveness, allowing you to take initiative-taking steps to address any areas of concern. Reflecting on these questions can help individuals gain insight into their tendency to make excuses and how it may be impacting their personal, professional, and commercial endeavors. It can also guide them towards adopting a more accountable and initiative-taking mindset in addressing challenges and pursuing their goals.

Q. Is "Denial" a cause that is preventing you, your team, department, or organisation from being effective?

1. No, I don't know anyone like that in my team or organsiation

2. Yes. It has been identified in the relevant individual(s).

3. On the case. Working to address it and improve effectiveness.

4. Oops. No, the action plan is not yet completed (or started).

5. This is concerning. I Need help with this – fast.

Ignorance (The Uninformed)

Ignorance, or "The Uninformed" as I term it, refers to lack of knowledge, insight, or awareness regarding concepts, situations or contexts that have a direct impact on our decision-making ability and capacity to respond appropriately. Ignorance breeds ineffectiveness by limiting our understanding of challenges, tools, best practices etc. that allow us to navigate difficulties successfully.

For instance, a leader ignoring emerging digital threats is crippled crafting defensive strategy. Without comprehending the nuances of new technologies disrupting their industry, organizations suffer inertia unable to reinvent offerings customers now desire. Ignorance constrains choices. It keeps us clinging to outdated paradigms even as the ground shifts seismically.

The root cause lies in assumptions of adequacy - overestimating how much we truly know. Ignorance persists by refusing to acknowledge the vastness of unknown unknowns. Even expertise in one domain cannot compensate lacking other interlocking perspectives. In rapidly evolving environments, the skill of continuously learning becomes mandatory.

Escaping ignorance requires humility acknowledging we don't know enough coupled with curiosity expanding horizons. Lifelong learning at scale using digital academy models arms us with robust mental models. Knowledge compounds unlocking genius able to calmly solve almost any storm. Thus prepared, we exit outdated environments of the uninformed into enlightened worlds brimming with possibility.

What the experts say.

Alan Kay, a renowned computer scientist known for his work in pioneering the development of the personal computer and graphical user interface. He made significant contributions to the fields of computer science and human-computer interaction. He once memorably stated - "Perspective is worth 80 IQ points".

Ignorance can be a significant barrier to success, hindering our ability to grow and achieve our goals. According to the author, John C. Maxwell, "The greatest enemy of knowledge is not ignorance, it is the illusion of knowledge."

This insightful quote highlights the danger of thinking we know everything when, we have much to learn.

Ignorance blinds us to opportunities for improvement and prevents us from seeking out latest information or perspectives. It can lead to costly mistakes and missed opportunities. By acknowledging our ignorance and embracing a mindset of continuous learning and growth, we can overcome this barrier and unlock our full potential for success.

Ever experienced a situation like these?

Imagine if the following had happened to you, how would you feel?

Amir, the head administrator at a hospital, underestimated the importance of cybersecurity measures, believing the hospital's systems were secure enough. Ignoring warnings about potential cyber threats and failing to invest in updated security protocols, Amir left the hospital vulnerable to cyberattacks. This ignorance resulted in a data breach compromising patient information, damaging the hospital's reputation, and exposing it to legal liabilities.

To rectify the situation, the hospital conducted a thorough audit of its cybersecurity infrastructure and policies. They invested in state-of-the-art cybersecurity solutions and provided training to staff on best practices for data protection. Amir underwent additional training on cybersecurity awareness and risk management. As a result, the hospital enhanced its cybersecurity posture, safeguarding patient data and restoring trust with stakeholders.

Another one:

Mike, the project manager for a construction firm, disregarded environmental regulations and community concerns when planning a new development project. Ignoring protests from environmental activists and objections from residents, Mike proceeded with the project without conducting proper environmental impact assessments. This ignorance led to legal disputes, delays in construction, and negative publicity, harming the firm's reputation and profitability.

To address the issue, the firm engaged with environmental experts and community stakeholders to assess the project's impact and address concerns. They revised the project plans to incorporate sustainable design principles and mitigate environmental risks. Mike received training on environmental compliance and stakeholder engagement. By prioritising environmental responsibility and community engagement, the construction firm regained public trust and successfully completed the project while minimising negative impacts.

My point?

In both scenarios, ignorance had detrimental effects on individuals, teams, and organizations, but initiative-taking measures such as education, collaboration, and policy changes helped rectify the situations and prevent future occurrences.

Ignorance refers to lack of insight, knowledge or awareness regarding concepts, contexts and forces relevant for informed analysis and decision making. It blindsides strategy by narrowing perspectives and restricting the lens through which we evaluate situations before responding.

Understanding Ignorance and its effects.

Ignorance can cast a shadow over confidence and performance like a dark cloud. Here are some signs that it's happening:

An individual might hesitate to take on new tasks or challenges because they lack the knowledge or skills to succeed, leading to missed opportunities for growth.

They might avoid seeking clarification or guidance out of fear of appearing ignorant, resulting in misunderstandings and errors. Ignorance can lead to consistent errors or poor performance in tasks that require specific knowledge or expertise.

A team affected by ignorance may exhibit low morale due to frustration or confusion stemming from a lack of understanding or direction. It can hinder effective communication within a team, leading to misunderstandings, conflicts, and inefficiencies.

When team members lack essential knowledge or skills, they may struggle to meet deadlines or achieve targets, impacting overall team performance.

Ignorance can lead to a decline in the quality of products or services offered by the organization, resulting in dissatisfied customers and damaged reputation. Ignorance of market trends or industry developments can also cause the organisation to fall behind competitors, leading to lost opportunities and decreased market share.

Employees may become disillusioned and leave the organization if they perceive a lack of support for learning and development, resulting in high turnover rates.

For me, signs of ignorance in the workplace can manifest in many ways, impacting confidence and performance at individual, team, and organizational levels. Recognizing these signs and taking initiative-taking steps to address knowledge gaps is essential for fostering a culture of continuous learning and improvement.

If it goes unchecked.

Unchecked ignorance can have significant negative impacts on individuals, teams, and organisations in a work environment:

- **Stunted Growth.** An individual's lack of awareness or understanding can hinder their personal and professional development, limiting opportunities for advancement and growth.

- **Low Self-Confidence.** Ignorance can erode an individual's confidence in their abilities, leading to self-doubt and a reluctance to take on new challenges or responsibilities.

- **Missed Opportunities.** Ignorance of industry trends or best practices can result in missed opportunities for career advancement or recognition.

- **Poor Collaboration.** Ignorance within a team can lead to misunderstandings, miscommunication, and ineffective collaboration, hindering progress on projects and goals.

- **Decreased Morale.** Team members may feel frustrated or demotivated when collaborating with ignorant colleagues who fail to contribute meaningfully or share necessary information.

- **Increased Conflict.** Ignorance can fuel conflict within a team as individuals may resist feedback or refuse to acknowledge their mistakes, leading to tension and resentment.

- **Diminished Performance.** Ignorance at the organizational level can result in subpar performance, missed targets, and decreased productivity, impacting the bottom line.

- **Reputational Damage.** Ignorance can tarnish an organization's reputation, leading to loss of trust from clients, customers, and stakeholders.

- **Lack of Innovation.** Ignorance of market trends or emerging technologies can hinder an organization's ability to innovate and adapt to changing circumstances, putting it at a disadvantage compared to competitors.

For me, unchecked ignorance can lead to detrimental outcomes for individuals, teams, and organizations, including limited growth opportunities, decreased morale, and diminished performance. Recognising and addressing ignorance through education, training, and a culture of continuous learning is crucial to fostering a productive and successful work environment.

Potential Solutions.

Here are seven preventative measures to combat ignorance in the workplace:

1. **Encourage Learning Culture.** Promote a culture of continuous learning where individuals are encouraged

to seek knowledge and expand their skills through training, workshops, and professional development opportunities.

2. **Provide Access to Resources.** Ensure individuals and teams have access to relevant resources such as books, online courses, and educational materials to stay informed and up to date in their respective fields.

3. **Facilitate Knowledge Sharing.** Create platforms or meetings where team members can share insights, experiences, and best practices to collectively enhance their understanding and expertise.

4. **Promote Curiosity.** Encourage individuals to ask questions, explore new ideas, and challenge assumptions to foster a mindset of curiosity and intellectual curiosity.

5. **Assign Coaches and Mentors.** Pair less experienced individuals with mentors or subject matter experts who can provide guidance, support, and knowledge transfer to help bridge knowledge gaps.

6. **Regular Assessments.** Conduct regular assessments or evaluations to identify areas where knowledge gaps exist and develop targeted learning plans to address them.

7. **Celebrate Learning Achievements.** Recognise and celebrate individuals and teams who actively pursue learning opportunities and demonstrate a commitment to personal and professional growth, reinforcing the value of knowledge acquisition and sharing.

By implementing these preventative measures, individuals, teams, and organisations can proactively combat ignorance and create an environment conducive to continuous learning, growth, and success.

Ask yourself:

Take a moment to ask yourself (or members of your team) the following questions about "Denial" to help evaluate your personal, professional, or commercial situation:

- Am I open to learning new things and exploring different perspectives, or do I tend to stick to what I already know?
- Do I actively seek out information and seek to understand topics outside of my comfort zone, or do I shy away from unfamiliar subjects?
- Am I proactive in staying updated on industry trends and advancements, or do I rely solely on my current knowledge and experience?
- Do I seek feedback from colleagues and supervisors to identify areas for improvement, or do I assume I know everything I need to know to succeed in my role?
- Is my business adaptable to changes in the market and customer preferences, or do we cling to outdated strategies and practices?
- Do we regularly evaluate our products, services, and processes to identify areas where we may be lacking knowledge or understanding?

These questions can help you assess whether ignorance might be impacting your personal growth, professional success, or business effectiveness, allowing you to take proactive steps to address any areas of concern. Reflecting on these questions can help individuals gain insight into their tendency to make excuses and how it may be impacting their personal, professional, and commercial endeavours.

Q. Is "Ignorance" a cause that is preventing you, your team, department, or organisation from being effective?

1.   No, I don't know anyone like that in my team or organsiation

2. Yes. It has been identified in the relevant individual(s).

3. On the case. Working to address it and improve effectiveness.

4. Oops. No, the action plan is not yet completed (or started).

5. This is concerning. I Need help with this – fast.

Apathy (The Uninspired)

Apathy, or "The Uninspired" as I term it, refers to a lack of motivation, passion, or interest in staff and individuals towards fellow staff, tasks, activities, and responsibilities where engagement is expected or required. Apathy encompasses a spectrum of emotions ranging from bored indifference all the way to frustration, futility, and active disengagement.

When apathetic, we feel detached and robotic rather than alive and enthusiastic. We struggle to focus, drag our feet completing tasks, and simply feel drained going through the motions. Previously exciting goals lost their sheen. Work becomes just a job rather than a calling. Even close relationships can suffer neglect under apathy's dull haze.

Left unchecked in teams and organisations, apathy becomes culturally embedded spawning a toxicity that rationalizes mediocrity. As engagement dwindles, innovation suffers, turf wars emerge and attrition increases. By tolerating lukewarm energies, companies surrender their capacity to excel.

What causes such demotivation to take hold even amongst talented, well-intentioned people? The reasons range from poor work-life balance, monotonous environments, activities misaligned from innate passions to lack of autonomy or inspiration. Once initiated however, apathy feeds on itself in downward spirals harder to reverse.

Individuals suffering from apathy need to rekindle their intrinsic fires of motivation or as I like to term, they need to get on point, on form and on fire. High achievers sustain lifelong zeal not through carrot-stick external pressures, but self-designed conditions engineering peak flow. Victory over apathy lies in institutionalising personal and organisational practices that foster engaged empowerment on demand.

What the experts say.

Apathy can function as a significant barrier to success, holding us back from reaching our full potential. In the words of American author and motivational speaker, Zig Ziglar, "The first step in solving a problem is to recognise that it does exist." This insightful quote underscores the importance of acknowledging apathy as a problem before we can begin to address it.

When we become indifferent or disengaged, we lose the drive and motivation needed to pursue our goals.

This lack of enthusiasm can hinder our progress and prevent us from taking the necessary actions to achieve success. By recognising and overcoming apathy, we can reignite our passion and drive, unlocking new opportunities for growth and fulfillment in our personal and professional lives.

Ever experienced a situation like these?

At a fast-paced tech startup, Kenny, a graphic designer, began to feel apathetic towards his project deadlines and team collaborations. He showed little interest in meeting project milestones or contributing innovative ideas, causing delays in product development, and frustrating his team members. This lack of enthusiasm affected team dynamics and jeopardized the organization's reputation for timely delivery.

To tackle the issue, the project manager organised team-building activities to foster a sense of camaraderie and shared purpose among team members. Kenny received personalised feedback and mentoring sessions to reignite his passion for software development and problem-solving. Additionally, the project manager implemented agile project management techniques to improve workflow efficiency and accountability. With a renewed sense of purpose and collaborative spirit, Kenny and the project team successfully met their project deadlines and delivered high-quality products to clients.

If not you, then maybe someone you know has experienced a situation like Lauren:

In a bustling retail store, Lauren, a sales associate, began to feel apathetic towards her job duties and customer interactions. She showed little interest in upselling products or providing excellent customer service, leading to a decline in sales and customer satisfaction. This lack of engagement affected the entire sales team's morale and impacted the store's profitability.

To address the situation, the store manager implemented regular team meetings to discuss sales goals and provide motivational training sessions. Lauren received one-on-one coaching to reignite her passion for customer service and sales. Additionally, the manager introduced incentive programs to reward top performers, encouraging healthy competition and boosting team motivation. With renewed focus and motivation, Lauren and the sales team improved their performance, resulting in increased sales and happier customers.

My Point?

In both scenarios, initiative-taking measures such as training, coaching, and team-building activities helped combat apathy and reinvigorate individuals and teams, leading to improved performance and organizational success.

Apathy and inertia are both factors that can hinder progress and effectiveness, but they arise from different mindsets and behaviours.

Apathy refers to a lack of interest, enthusiasm, or concern towards one's responsibilities or goals. It involves a sense of indifference or disengagement, where individuals may show little motivation or initiative to take action or make improvements. Apathy often results in inaction and can lead to stagnation and missed opportunities.

Inertia on the other hand refers to a tendency to resist change or remain in a state of rest or motion unless acted upon by an external force. It involves a reluctance or unwillingness to move or take action, even when it may be necessary or beneficial. Inertia can stem from fear of the unknown, complacency, or a preference for maintaining the status quo.

While both apathy and inertia can impede progress, apathy refers to a lack of interest, enthusiasm, or concern towards one's responsibilities, goals, or surroundings. It is characterized by a sense of indifference or disengagement, where individuals may show little motivation or initiative to take action or make improvements.

Apathy can manifest in various aspects of life, including personal relationships, work, and community involvement. It acts as a barrier to success by inhibiting productivity, stifling creativity, and hindering personal growth. Apathy prevents individuals from fully engaging with their tasks, leading to subpar performance, and missed opportunities for achievement. Recognizing and addressing apathy is essential for fostering an initiative-taking and motivated mindset conducive to success and fulfilment.

Understanding Apathy and its effects.

Let's explore how apathy can manifest in various industries and impact performance.

In the retail industry, a sales associate may show little enthusiasm when interacting with customers, failing to provide personalized assistance or upsell products. Team members lack motivation during sales meetings, contributing minimal ideas or feedback for improving customer experience. Sales metrics show a decline in customer satisfaction scores and revenue due to lacklustre customer interactions.

In the education sector, a teacher may display indifference towards lesson planning and classroom engagement, resulting in disinterested students and low academic performance.

Faculty members show little interest in collaborating on curriculum development or participating in professional development workshops. Student feedback may indicate decreased engagement and satisfaction, leading to declining enrolment rates and reputational damage.

In the Healthcare field, a nurse may exhibit apathy towards patient care, neglecting to provide thorough assessments or follow-up care. Healthcare professionals may display lack of motivation during team meetings, resulting in decreased efficiency and communication breakdowns.

Patient satisfaction surveys reveal dissatisfaction with the quality of care provided, leading to decreased patient retention and potential legal issues.

In each scenario, apathy negatively affects individuals, teams, and organisations, resulting in decreased performance, morale, and success. Recognising and addressing signs of apathy through motivation strategies, training programs, and fostering a positive work culture is essential to mitigate its impact and promote overall productivity and effectiveness.

If it goes unchecked.

Imagine a workplace where apathy is left unchecked, like a

slow leak draining energy and enthusiasm. Here's how it could affect individuals, teams, and the organization:

- **Lack of Fulfilment.** An individual may feel unfulfilled and disengaged from their work, leading to decreased motivation and satisfaction.

- **Stagnation.** Without a drive to improve or excel, the individual may become stagnant in their role, hindering their personal and professional growth.

- **Career Stagnation.** Apathy can prevent individuals from pursuing new opportunities or advancing in their careers, resulting in missed chances for advancement and fulfilment.

- **Diminished Collaboration.** Apathetic team members may contribute minimally to group projects or discussions, leading to decreased collaboration and innovation.

- **Negative Atmosphere.** A team affected by apathy may experience low morale and a negative atmosphere, making it challenging to foster creativity and productivity.

- **Decreased Productivity.** With team members lacking motivation, productivity may suffer as tasks take longer to complete and deadlines are missed.

- **Decline in Performance.** Apathy across the organization can lead to a decline in overall performance and productivity, impacting the bottom line.

- **Loss of Reputation.** Apathetic employees may deliver subpar service or products, resulting in dissatisfied customers and damage to the organization's reputation.

- **High Labour Turnover.** Employees may become disillusioned and seek opportunities elsewhere if they feel their contributions are not valued, leading to increased turnover rates and loss of talent.

For me, unchecked apathy can have far-reaching consequences, affecting individuals, teams, and the organisation. Recognising and addressing apathy early is essential to fostering a positive work environment and maintaining productivity and success.

Potential Solutions.

To prevent apathy from taking hold, individuals, teams, and organisations can take initiative-taking measures:

1. **Set Clear Goals,** establishing clear and achievable goals can provide individuals with a sense of purpose and direction, reducing the likelihood of apathy.

2. **Provide Meaningful Work.** Assign tasks that align with individuals' interests and skills, fostering a sense of fulfilment and motivation.

3. **Encourage Open Communication.** Create an environment where individuals feel comfortable expressing concerns and seeking support, fostering a sense of belonging and engagement.

4. **Offer Recognition and Rewards.** Recognise and reward individuals for their contributions and achievements, reinforcing their value to the team and organization.

5. **Promote Work-Life Balance**. Encourage individuals to maintain a healthy balance between work and personal life to prevent burnout and maintain enthusiasm for their work.

6. **Invest in Training and Development.** Provide opportunities for skill development and career advancement to keep individuals engaged and motivated to learn and grow.

7. **Foster a Positive Culture.** Cultivate a positive and supportive work culture that values teamwork, creativity, and innovation, inspiring individuals to stay committed and enthusiastic about their work.

By implementing these preventative measures, individuals, teams, and organisations can proactively combat apathy and create an environment conducive to continuous learning, growth, and success.

Ask yourself:

Take a moment to ask yourself (or members of your team) the following questions about "apathy" to help evaluate your personal, professional, or commercial situation:

- Do I often feel disinterested or unmotivated in pursuing my goals or hobbies?
- Am I finding it challenging to maintain enthusiasm and energy in my daily activities?
- Do I frequently procrastinate or feel indifferent towards tasks and projects at work?
- Am I lacking enthusiasm or initiative in seeking opportunities for advancement or skill development?
- Do I feel indifferent towards the success or failure of my business ventures or projects?
- Am I neglecting customer feedback or market trends due to a lack of interest or motivation?

These questions can help you reflect on whether apathy may be affecting your personal growth, professional success, or business effectiveness. Recognising and addressing any signs of apathy early on can help you regain motivation, engagement, and drive to get on point, on form and on fire towards achieving your goals.

Q. Is "Apathy" a cause that is preventing you, your team, department, or organisation from being effective?

1. No, I don't know anyone like that in my team or organsiation

2. Yes.   It has been identified in the relevant individual(s).

3. On the case. Working to address it and improve effectiveness.

4. Oops. No, the action plan is not yet completed (or started).

5. This is concerning.   I Need help with this – fast.

Fear (The Frozen)

Among the most restricting forces that hold people back from effectiveness is the cause I term "The Frozen" - otherwise known as fear. Fear creates a frigid emotional state that inhibits growth, creativity, and achievement. When we allow fear to dictate our choices, it traps our talents in a frozen cage of risk-aversion and self-doubt.

The icy grip of fear manifests in many forms - anxiety about the future, dread of failure, worries over subordinates' judgments, and concern over known and unknown dangers all contribute. Regardless of its origin, fear frosts over our potentiality and productivity. It strangles our willingness to learn, to try, to trust in ourselves and in others around us. Frozen by fear, we opt for inaction over action, stagnancy over change, and the comfortable over the challenging.

In our icy mental bunkers formed of fear, we rationalise away opportunities for growth. We prefer the cold but predictable to facing the necessary heat that comes with fresh challenges and new directions. And thus, our talents, creativity, and highest potentials lie locked away, frozen by our inability to thaw our fears and break out of our emotional shells.

The path beyond fear lies in courage and boldness.

Courage provides the heat source necessary to melt our icy hesitation. When we face fear with bravery powered by vision and self-confidence, we emancipate our talents to take flight. By boldly confronting what holds them hostage, we grant our gifts the power to soar well beyond the frozen cage.

In this chapter on fear, we unravel one of the most underestimated yet potent forces stalling individuals and organisations from reaching their highest potentials - both materially and spiritually. By evolution's design, fear protected us from wild beasts and warring tribes in bygone eras, but left unchecked in the modern world, fear often keeps us playing small without any tangible demons to battle besides phantoms within our own minds taunting us with projected losses.

You will learn how fear shrinks possibility into anxiety starting from biological impulses. But more potently, complex psychological and social dynamics conspire to feed cultures mired in groupthink today through risk-aversion and perfectionism norms. By peering into fear-based thinking plaguing workplaces and communities, often cloaked in positivity glosses, we expose vast swathes of muted talents and stalled innovations underlying stagnation across many industries today.

What the experts say.

"Fear can be a powerful force that holds us back from reaching our full potential," explains motivational speaker and author Brian Tracy in his book "No Excuses! The Power of Self-Discipline." He emphasises, *"Fear is the main reason why people fail to achieve their goals and fulfil their potential."*

This insightful quote underscores the significant impact fear can have on our success. Whether it's fear of failure, rejection, or the unknown, it can paralyze us and prevent us from taking action towards our goals. Fear creates barriers that limit our growth and opportunities for success. It keeps us stuck in our comfort zones, unwilling to take risks or step outside of familiarity.

Overcoming fear requires courage and resilience. As Tracy suggests, *"The key to conquering fear is to face it head-on and take action despite the discomfort."* By confronting our fears and pushing past them, we can unlock our true potential and achieve greater success in life.

Ever experienced a situation like this?

In a hotel, Stephanie, a front desk receptionist, experienced fear of handling difficult guest complaints. Her fear of confrontation and displeasing guests led her to avoid addressing issues promptly and effectively. As a result, guest satisfaction scores declined, leading to negative online reviews and a tarnished reputation for the hotel.

To address the situation, the hotel provided Stephanie with conflict resolution training and empowered her to escalate issues to management when necessary. They also implemented a system for regular feedback and coaching to help Stephanie build confidence in handling challenging situations. Additionally, the hotel offered incentives for staff who received positive guest feedback. Through support and training, Stephanie gradually overcame her fear and became more adept at handling guest concerns, leading to improved guest satisfaction, online reviews, and a positive reputation for the hotel.

If not you, then maybe someone you know has experienced a situation like this, because.

Some people are simply mistrusting, distrusting and even fearful of MarTech and AI.

In a transportation company, the logistics team faced fear of adopting new technology, AI (Artificial intelligence) and processes due to concerns about job security and unfamiliarity with new systems. This fear of change led to resistance and reluctance to embrace efficiency improvements, resulting in delays in shipments and increased operational costs.

To address the issue, the company provided comprehensive

training on AI, the new technology platform, and processes, emphasising the benefits for both employees and the organisation. They also implemented a change management strategy that included clear communication, stakeholder involvement, and gradual implementation to ease fears and build acceptance.

Additionally, the company offered incentives for employees who demonstrated proficiency with the new systems. By addressing fears and providing support, the company successfully transitioned to the new processes, leading to improved efficiency, cost savings, and employee morale.

My point?

In both scenarios, addressing fear through supportive measures, training, and creating a culture of psychological safety allowed individuals and teams to overcome obstacles and perform at their best, benefiting the organisation.

Fear often acts as a smokescreen clouding our confidence. It leads us to abandon our truth by contraction. We question our intuition and worth.

Fear feeds on uncertainty about the future. It makes unknown outcomes appear ominous. With roots in a basic human instinct for self-preservation and safety in numbers, fear triggers when we perceive risks of loss - whether loss of security, resources, relationships, respect or even ego.

Our threat response floods our system with cortisol and adrenaline, narrowing focus. While this helps us survive real perils, it often misfires today, miring us in anxious what-ifs even without tangible danger.

Some say fear stands for False Evidence Appearing Real. Me? I say Fear is all about Fostering Empowerment, Achievement & Resilience.

Understanding Fear and its effects.

When gripped by fear, we shrink back from risks that could lead to growth. We avoid changes that disrupt our comfort zone or challenge status quos anchoring our sense of safety. Though these feelings of trepidation protect us from immediate harm, they often hold us back habitually when no real danger exists. We become frozen by phantoms of our own making. Consider the project manager afraid of rejecting scope creep who waters down deliverables. Or the star performer terrified of demanding a promotion and being denied.

Fear acts as a smokescreen clouding our confidence. It leads us to abandon our truth by contraction. We question our intuition and worth. Fear feeds on uncertainty about the future. It makes unknown outcomes appear ominous. With roots in a basic human instinct for self-preservation and safety in numbers, fear triggers when we perceive risks of loss - whether loss of security, resources, relationships, respect or even ego.

At its core, fear stems from disconnect - from own worth and from life's meaning beyond achievements, assets, or admiration.

In a work environment, various signs and indicators may manifest and indicate that fear is impacting performance at various levels, including:

- **Avoidance Behaviour.** An individual may avoid taking on new tasks or responsibilities due to fear of failure or criticism.

- **Procrastination.** Constant delays in completing tasks or making decisions can signal fear of making mistakes or facing consequences.

- **Physical Symptoms.** Visible signs of stress such as nervousness, sweating, or fidgeting may indicate underlying fear.

- **Lack of Collaboration.** Team members may hesitate to share ideas or offer feedback during meetings due to fear of judgment or conflict.

- **Low Morale.** A pervasive sense of unease or tension among team members can suggest an environment where fear is prevalent.

- **Decreased Productivity.** Fear-driven teams may experience a decline in productivity as individuals focus more on avoiding mistakes than on achieving goals.

- **High Labour Turnover.** A higher-than-average turnover rate may indicate that employees are leaving due to a fear-based culture or management style.

- **Resistance to Change.** Organisational inertia or reluctance to adopt new practices could stem from fear of the unknown or fear of failure.

- **Poor Performance.** Overall declines in performance metrics such as sales figures or customer satisfaction scores may be linked to fear-induced behaviours at various levels.

Identifying these signs early on is crucial for addressing underlying fears and fostering a more supportive and positive work environment conducive to individual and organizational success.

If it goes unchecked.

The existence of fear or a culture of fear in the workplace can have detrimental effects on individuals, teams, and the organisation, including:

- **Stagnated Growth.** Fear may prevent individuals from taking on new challenges or pursuing opportunities for growth and development, leading to stagnation in their careers.
- **Diminished Confidence.** Constant fear of making mistakes or facing criticism can erode an individual's self-confidence, hindering their ability to perform at their best.
- **Physical and Mental Health Issues.** Prolonged exposure to fear and stress in the workplace can lead to adverse health effects such as anxiety, depression, and burnout.
- **Dysfunctional Dynamics.** A culture of fear can create an atmosphere of distrust and competition among team members, undermining collaboration, and teamwork.
- **Decreased Morale.** Fear-driven environments often result in low morale, as team members feel demotivated and disengaged from their work.
- **Communication Breakdowns.** Fear can inhibit open and honest communication within teams, leading to misunderstandings, conflicts, and breakdowns in communication channels.
- **Decreased Productivity.** Fear can lead to decreased productivity as employees focus more on avoiding mistakes or repercussions than on achieving organizational goals.
- **Increased Labour Turnover.** A culture of fear often results in high churn rate of staff as employees seek to escape a toxic work environment, leading to loss of talent and increased recruitment costs.
- **Negative Reputation.** Organisations with a reputation for fostering fear may struggle to attract top talent and retain customers, leading to long-term damage to their brand and competitiveness in the market.

Overall, unchecked fear or a culture of fear can have far-reaching consequences, impacting not only individual well-being but also team dynamics and organisational success. Recognizing and addressing fear-related issues is essential for creating a healthy and supportive work environment conducive to growth, innovation, and success.

Potential Solutions.

To prevent a fear culture from taking hold, individuals, teams, and organisations can take initiative-taking measures, such as:

1. **Promote Open Communication.** Encourage individuals to express their concerns and fears openly without fear of judgment or reprisal.

2. **Provide Support and Resources.** Offer training, mentorship, and counselling services to help individuals develop coping mechanisms and resilience in the face of fear.

3. **Set Realistic Expectations.** Establish clear goals and expectations for individuals and teams to reduce uncertainty and alleviate anxiety.

4. **Foster a Positive Work Environment.** Create a culture of trust, collaboration, and psychological safety where employees feel valued, supported, and respected.

5. **Encourage Risk-Taking.** Celebrate initiative and innovation, even if it involves the risk of failure, to promote a growth mindset and mitigate fear of taking chances.

6. **Offer Feedback and Recognition.** Provide regular feedback and recognition for achievements to boost confidence and motivation, reducing fear of failure or inadequacy.

7. **Lead by Example.** Demonstrate courage and resilience in the face of challenges, inspiring others to confront their fears and persevere through tricky situations.

By implementing these preventative measures, individuals, teams, and organizations can create a supportive and empowering environment that mitigates the effects of fear and fosters personal and professional growth.

Ask yourself:

Take a moment to reflect and ask yourself (or members of your team) the following questions about "fear" and the existence of a fear culture to help evaluate your personal, professional, or commercial situation:

- Do I often feel anxious or hesitant to take risks in my personal life due to fear of failure or rejection?
- Am I avoiding opportunities for growth or personal development because of fear?
- Do I feel intimidated or fearful of expressing my ideas or opinions in the workplace?
- Am I hesitant to confront issues or challenges at work due to fear of conflict or

  reprisal?

- Do I notice a pervasive atmosphere of fear or apprehension among colleagues or employees in my business?
- Are decisions in my business driven more by fear of failure than by strategic planning and innovation?
- Do I lead with transparency and openness, or do I rule through fear and intimidation?
- Am I fostering a culture of trust and empowerment, or is fear undermining morale and productivity in my team or organization?

Reflecting on these questions can help you and others in your team or organization decide whether fear be impacting their personal, professional, and commercial lives. Recognizing and addressing fear-related issues is crucial for fostering a healthy and supportive environment conducive to growth, innovation, and success.

Q. Is "Fear" a cause that is preventing you, your team, department, or organisation from being effective?

1. No, I don't know anyone like that in my team or organsiation

2. Yes.   It has been identified in the relevant individual(s).

3. On the case. Working to address it and improve effectiveness.

4. Oops. No, the action plan is not yet completed (or started).

5. This is concerning. I Need help with this – fast.

Thank You

As we wrap up our journey through the seven causes of highly ineffective people (and how to address them), I want to take a moment to thank you for joining me on this journey. I also ask you to reflect on the insights I have shared and the transformative potential that lies ahead. Throughout our exploration, we've delved into the depths of ego, blame, excuses, denial, ignorance, apathy, and fear — all formidable barriers standing between us and our goals.

Re-Read. Relate. Assimilate & apply.

It can pay great dividends to re-read the book and complete each of the exercises and activities. Tor armed with knowledge and determination, you have the power to overcome these obstacles and unlock your full potential. Addressing each cause offers us a pathway to growth and self-discovery.

In writing this book, my greatest hope is that you've found resonance in these words, that you've recognised aspects of yourself (or your team) and your experiences within these pages. For in that recognition lies the seed of transformation — the seed of possibility.

I urge you to take these insights to heart, to assimilate them into your daily life, and to apply them with unwavering commitment. Whether you're striving for personal excellence, fostering a thriving team dynamic, or leading an organisation to new heights, the principles outlined here hold the key to your success.

Imagine a world where fear no longer paralyses us, where denial gives way to acceptance, where apathy is replaced by passion, and excuses are transformed into action. Picture the scene where ego takes a backseat to collaboration, where ignorance is replaced by curiosity, and where inertia gives way to momentum.

This is the world that awaits us – a world of limitless potential and boundless opportunity. But to reach it, we must be willing to take the first step, to embrace the journey with courage and conviction. So, dear reader, remember this: the power to change lies within each of us.

Afterall, you already have the power, you just need reminding occasionally how to use it and breakthrough the barriers of personal and professional success.

Here's to getting on point, on form, and on fire, one step at a time. Remember if you need help, or have questions, then get in touch. Let's make your next 12 months, the best you've ever had.

With hope and anticipation,

Fraser J. Hay

One Last Thing...

Have you found **value** and **benefit** from reading this book and in being introduced to different ways to unify and simplify the management of your marketing?

Do you think others struggling with marketing ideas would find a **benefit** from reading this book if they didn't know about the software solutions I share?

Would you be prepared to **recommend** my book to others, or be prepared to write a positive review about it?

Who would be the first two people that you know that might be struggling with one or a combination of the causes and barriers we've discussed, who might benefit from reading this book?

Feel free to direct them to my book. I really do hope you have gotten value from my book. You will if you choose to act and start making changes to your marketing approach with the ideas I've shared.

Take a moment, reflect on this book, and write down the top 5 key "takeaways" you've gained from this book. Write what you've learned and consider adding a review of the book, for amazing things are about to start happening when you begin embracing and applying the principles contained herein, and my other books.

Even better, add a video review or testimonial and ping me the URL and in return I'll give you a wee personal thank you.

In addition to adding a review, consider sharing your thoughts via your online networks such as LinkedIn, Facebook, and X (twitter). If you believe what you've read is worth sharing, then please would you take a few seconds to let your colleagues know about it? If it can have a positive impact on their life or work, they'll be incredibly grateful to you.

And remember, if you've got questions, then please do get in touch.

Fraser J Hay

www.itstacksup.com

FREE BONUS

As a thank you for reading my book, I also invite you to sign up to one of my free webinars available on my website at www.itstacksup.com

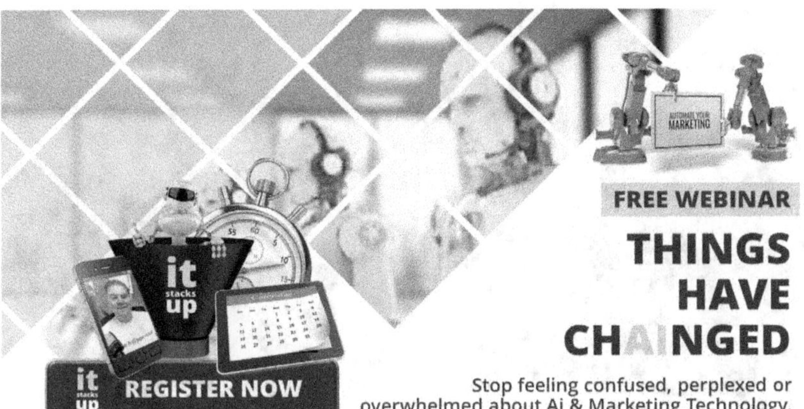
AUTOMATE YOUR MARKETING
FREE WEBINAR
THINGS HAVE CHAINGED
Stop feeling confused, perplexed or overwhelmed about Ai & Marketing Technology.
it stacks up
REGISTER NOW
Sign Up for FREE at www.itstacksup.com

FREE WEBINAR
90 MINUTE MARKETING PLAN
" Fast paced, challenging & Highly Recommended. "
it stacks up
REGISTER NOW
Sign Up for FREE at www.itstacksup.com

Any questions? Then visit www.itstacksup.com.